KEEP ORGANIZED PASSWORD BOOK

PASSWORD REMINDER BOOK

ACTIVINOTES

Activinotes

DAILY JOURNALS, PLANNERS, NOTEBOOKS AND OTHER BLANK BOOKS

WEBSITE URL: _____

USERNAME: _____

PASSWORD: _____

HINT: _____

NOTES: _____

_____

WEBSITE URL: _____

USERNAME: _____

PASSWORD: _____

HINT: _____

NOTES: _____

_____

WEBSITE URL: _____

USERNAME: _____

PASSWORD: _____

HINT: _____

NOTES: _____

_____

WEBSITE URL: _____

USERNAME: _____

PASSWORD: _____

HINT: _____

NOTES: _____

_____

WEBSITE URL: _____

USERNAME: _____

PASSWORD: _____

HINT: _____

NOTES: _____

_____

WEBSITE URL: _____

USERNAME: _____

PASSWORD: _____

HINT: _____

NOTES: _____

_____

WEBSITE URL: _____

USERNAME: _____

PASSWORD: _____

HINT: _____

NOTES: _____

_____

WEBSITE URL: _____

USERNAME: _____

PASSWORD: _____

HINT: _____

NOTES: _____

_____

_____

WEBSITE URL: _____

USERNAME: _____

PASSWORD: _____

HINT: _____

NOTES: _____

_____

WEBSITE URL: _____

USERNAME: _____

PASSWORD: _____

HINT: _____

NOTES: _____

_____

WEBSITE URL: _____

USERNAME: _____

PASSWORD: _____

HINT: _____

NOTES: _____

_____

WEBSITE URL: _____

USERNAME: _____

PASSWORD: _____

HINT: _____

NOTES: _____

_____

_____

WEBSITE URL: _____

USERNAME: _____

PASSWORD: _____

HINT: _____

NOTES: _____

_____

WEBSITE URL: _____

USERNAME: _____

PASSWORD: _____

HINT: _____

NOTES: _____

_____

WEBSITE URL: _____

USERNAME: _____

PASSWORD: _____

HINT: _____

NOTES: _____

_____

WEBSITE URL: _____

USERNAME: _____

PASSWORD: _____

HINT: _____

NOTES: _____

_____

_____

WEBSITE URL: _____

USERNAME: _____

PASSWORD: _____

HINT: _____

NOTES: _____

_____

WEBSITE URL: _____

USERNAME: _____

PASSWORD: _____

HINT: _____

NOTES: _____

_____

WEBSITE URL: _____

USERNAME: _____

PASSWORD: _____

HINT: _____

NOTES: _____

_____

WEBSITE URL: _____

USERNAME: _____

PASSWORD: _____

HINT: _____

NOTES: _____

_____

_____

WEBSITE URL: _____

USERNAME: _____

PASSWORD: _____

HINT: _____

NOTES: _____

_____

WEBSITE URL: _____

USERNAME: _____

PASSWORD: _____

HINT: _____

NOTES: _____

_____

WEBSITE URL: _____

USERNAME: _____

PASSWORD: _____

HINT: _____

NOTES: _____

_____

WEBSITE URL: _____

USERNAME: _____

PASSWORD: _____

HINT: _____

NOTES: _____

_____

_____

WEBSITE URL: _____

USERNAME: _____

PASSWORD: _____

HINT: _____

NOTES: _____

_____

WEBSITE URL: _____

USERNAME: _____

PASSWORD: _____

HINT: _____

NOTES: _____

_____

WEBSITE URL: _____

USERNAME: _____

PASSWORD: _____

HINT: _____

NOTES: _____

_____

WEBSITE URL: _____

USERNAME: _____

PASSWORD: _____

HINT: _____

NOTES: _____

_____

_____

WEBSITE URL: _____

USERNAME: _____

PASSWORD: _____

HINT: _____

NOTES: _____

_____

WEBSITE URL: _____

USERNAME: _____

PASSWORD: _____

HINT: _____

NOTES: _____

_____

WEBSITE URL: _____

USERNAME: _____

PASSWORD: _____

HINT: _____

NOTES: _____

_____

WEBSITE URL: _____

USERNAME: _____

PASSWORD: _____

HINT: _____

NOTES: _____

_____

_____

WEBSITE URL: _____

USERNAME: _____

PASSWORD: _____

HINT: _____

NOTES: _____

_____

WEBSITE URL: _____

USERNAME: _____

PASSWORD: _____

HINT: _____

NOTES: _____

_____

WEBSITE URL: _____

USERNAME: _____

PASSWORD: _____

HINT: _____

NOTES: _____

_____

WEBSITE URL: _____

USERNAME: _____

PASSWORD: _____

HINT: _____

NOTES: _____

_____

_____

WEBSITE URL: _____

USERNAME: _____

PASSWORD: _____

HINT: _____

NOTES: _____

_____

WEBSITE URL: _____

USERNAME: _____

PASSWORD: _____

HINT: _____

NOTES: _____

_____

WEBSITE URL: _____

USERNAME: _____

PASSWORD: _____

HINT: _____

NOTES: _____

_____

WEBSITE URL: _____

USERNAME: _____

PASSWORD: _____

HINT: _____

NOTES: _____

_____

_____

WEBSITE URL: _____

USERNAME: _____

PASSWORD: _____

HINT: _____

NOTES: _____

_____

WEBSITE URL: _____

USERNAME: _____

PASSWORD: _____

HINT: _____

NOTES: _____

_____

WEBSITE URL: _____

USERNAME: _____

PASSWORD: _____

HINT: _____

NOTES: _____

_____

WEBSITE URL: _____

USERNAME: _____

PASSWORD: _____

HINT: _____

NOTES: _____

_____

_____

WEBSITE URL: _____

USERNAME: _____

PASSWORD: _____

HINT: _____

NOTES: _____

_____

WEBSITE URL: _____

USERNAME: _____

PASSWORD: _____

HINT: _____

NOTES: _____

_____

WEBSITE URL: _____

USERNAME: _____

PASSWORD: _____

HINT: _____

NOTES: _____

_____

WEBSITE URL: _____

USERNAME: _____

PASSWORD: _____

HINT: _____

NOTES: _____

_____

_____

WEBSITE URL: _____

USERNAME: _____

PASSWORD: _____

HINT: _____

NOTES: _____

_____

WEBSITE URL: _____

USERNAME: _____

PASSWORD: _____

HINT: _____

NOTES: _____

_____

WEBSITE URL: _____

USERNAME: _____

PASSWORD: _____

HINT: _____

NOTES: _____

_____

WEBSITE URL: _____

USERNAME: _____

PASSWORD: _____

HINT: _____

NOTES: _____

_____

_____

WEBSITE URL: _____

USERNAME: _____

PASSWORD: _____

HINT: _____

NOTES: _____

_____

WEBSITE URL: _____

USERNAME: _____

PASSWORD: _____

HINT: _____

NOTES: _____

_____

WEBSITE URL: _____

USERNAME: _____

PASSWORD: _____

HINT: _____

NOTES: _____

_____

WEBSITE URL: _____

USERNAME: _____

PASSWORD: _____

HINT: _____

NOTES: _____

_____

_____

WEBSITE URL: _____

USERNAME: _____

PASSWORD: _____

HINT: _____

NOTES: _____

_____

WEBSITE URL: _____

USERNAME: _____

PASSWORD: _____

HINT: _____

NOTES: _____

_____

WEBSITE URL: _____

USERNAME: _____

PASSWORD: _____

HINT: _____

NOTES: _____

_____

WEBSITE URL: _____

USERNAME: _____

PASSWORD: _____

HINT: _____

NOTES: _____

_____

_____

WEBSITE URL: _____

USERNAME: _____

PASSWORD: _____

HINT: _____

NOTES: _____

_____

WEBSITE URL: _____

USERNAME: _____

PASSWORD: _____

HINT: _____

NOTES: _____

_____

WEBSITE URL: _____

USERNAME: _____

PASSWORD: _____

HINT: _____

NOTES: _____

_____

WEBSITE URL: _____

USERNAME: _____

PASSWORD: _____

HINT: _____

NOTES: _____

_____

_____

WEBSITE URL: _____

USERNAME: _____

PASSWORD: _____

HINT: _____

NOTES: _____

_____

WEBSITE URL: _____

USERNAME: _____

PASSWORD: _____

HINT: _____

NOTES: _____

_____

WEBSITE URL: _____

USERNAME: _____

PASSWORD: _____

HINT: _____

NOTES: _____

_____

WEBSITE URL: _____

USERNAME: _____

PASSWORD: _____

HINT: _____

NOTES: _____

_____

_____

WEBSITE URL: _____

USERNAME: _____

PASSWORD: _____

HINT: _____

NOTES: _____

_____

WEBSITE URL: _____

USERNAME: _____

PASSWORD: _____

HINT: _____

NOTES: _____

_____

WEBSITE URL: _____

USERNAME: _____

PASSWORD: _____

HINT: _____

NOTES: _____

_____

WEBSITE URL: _____

USERNAME: _____

PASSWORD: _____

HINT: _____

NOTES: _____

_____

_____

WEBSITE URL: _____

USERNAME: _____

PASSWORD: _____

HINT: _____

NOTES: _____

_____

WEBSITE URL: _____

USERNAME: _____

PASSWORD: _____

HINT: _____

NOTES: _____

_____

WEBSITE URL: _____

USERNAME: _____

PASSWORD: _____

HINT: _____

NOTES: _____

_____

WEBSITE URL: _____

USERNAME: _____

PASSWORD: _____

HINT: _____

NOTES: _____

_____

_____

WEBSITE URL: _____

USERNAME: _____

PASSWORD: _____

HINT: _____

NOTES: _____

_____

WEBSITE URL: _____

USERNAME: _____

PASSWORD: _____

HINT: _____

NOTES: _____

_____

WEBSITE URL: _____

USERNAME: _____

PASSWORD: _____

HINT: _____

NOTES: _____

_____

WEBSITE URL: _____

USERNAME: _____

PASSWORD: _____

HINT: _____

NOTES: _____

_____

_____

WEBSITE URL: _____

USERNAME: _____

PASSWORD: _____

HINT: _____

NOTES: _____

_____

WEBSITE URL: _____

USERNAME: _____

PASSWORD: _____

HINT: _____

NOTES: _____

_____

WEBSITE URL: _____

USERNAME: _____

PASSWORD: _____

HINT: _____

NOTES: _____

_____

WEBSITE URL: _____

USERNAME: _____

PASSWORD: _____

HINT: _____

NOTES: _____

_____

WEBSITE URL: _____

USERNAME: _____

PASSWORD: _____

HINT: _____

NOTES: _____

_____

WEBSITE URL: _____

USERNAME: _____

PASSWORD: _____

HINT: _____

NOTES: _____

_____

WEBSITE URL: _____

USERNAME: _____

PASSWORD: _____

HINT: _____

NOTES: _____

_____

WEBSITE URL: _____

USERNAME: _____

PASSWORD: _____

HINT: _____

NOTES: _____

_____

_____

WEBSITE URL: _____

USERNAME: _____

PASSWORD: _____

HINT: _____

NOTES: _____

_____

WEBSITE URL: _____

USERNAME: _____

PASSWORD: _____

HINT: _____

NOTES: _____

_____

WEBSITE URL: _____

USERNAME: _____

PASSWORD: _____

HINT: _____

NOTES: _____

_____

WEBSITE URL: _____

USERNAME: _____

PASSWORD: _____

HINT: _____

NOTES: _____

_____

_____

WEBSITE URL: _____

USERNAME: _____

PASSWORD: _____

HINT: _____

NOTES: _____

_____

WEBSITE URL: _____

USERNAME: _____

PASSWORD: _____

HINT: _____

NOTES: _____

_____

WEBSITE URL: _____

USERNAME: _____

PASSWORD: _____

HINT: _____

NOTES: _____

_____

WEBSITE URL: _____

USERNAME: _____

PASSWORD: _____

HINT: _____

NOTES: _____

_____

_____

WEBSITE URL: _____

USERNAME: _____

PASSWORD: _____

HINT: _____

NOTES: _____

_____

WEBSITE URL: _____

USERNAME: _____

PASSWORD: _____

HINT: _____

NOTES: _____

_____

WEBSITE URL: _____

USERNAME: _____

PASSWORD: _____

HINT: _____

NOTES: _____

_____

WEBSITE URL: _____

USERNAME: _____

PASSWORD: _____

HINT: _____

NOTES: _____

_____

_____

WEBSITE URL: _____

USERNAME: _____

PASSWORD: _____

HINT: _____

NOTES: _____

_____

WEBSITE URL: _____

USERNAME: _____

PASSWORD: _____

HINT: _____

NOTES: _____

_____

WEBSITE URL: _____

USERNAME: _____

PASSWORD: _____

HINT: _____

NOTES: _____

_____

WEBSITE URL: _____

USERNAME: _____

PASSWORD: _____

HINT: _____

NOTES: _____

_____

_____

WEBSITE URL: _____

USERNAME: _____

PASSWORD: _____

HINT: _____

NOTES: _____

_____

WEBSITE URL: _____

USERNAME: _____

PASSWORD: _____

HINT: _____

NOTES: _____

_____

WEBSITE URL: _____

USERNAME: _____

PASSWORD: _____

HINT: _____

NOTES: _____

_____

WEBSITE URL: _____

USERNAME: _____

PASSWORD: _____

HINT: _____

NOTES: _____

_____

_____

WEBSITE URL: _____

USERNAME: _____

PASSWORD: _____

HINT: _____

NOTES: _____

_____

WEBSITE URL: _____

USERNAME: _____

PASSWORD: _____

HINT: _____

NOTES: _____

_____

WEBSITE URL: _____

USERNAME: _____

PASSWORD: _____

HINT: _____

NOTES: _____

_____

WEBSITE URL: _____

USERNAME: _____

PASSWORD: _____

HINT: _____

NOTES: _____

_____

WEBSITE URL: _____

USERNAME: _____

PASSWORD: _____

HINT: _____

NOTES: _____

_____

WEBSITE URL: _____

USERNAME: _____

PASSWORD: _____

HINT: _____

NOTES: _____

_____

WEBSITE URL: _____

USERNAME: _____

PASSWORD: _____

HINT: _____

NOTES: _____

_____

WEBSITE URL: _____

USERNAME: _____

PASSWORD: _____

HINT: _____

NOTES: _____

_____

WEBSITE URL: _____

USERNAME: _____

PASSWORD: _____

HINT: _____

NOTES: _____

_____

WEBSITE URL: _____

USERNAME: _____

PASSWORD: _____

HINT: _____

NOTES: _____

_____

WEBSITE URL: _____

USERNAME: _____

PASSWORD: _____

HINT: _____

NOTES: _____

_____

WEBSITE URL: _____

USERNAME: _____

PASSWORD: _____

HINT: _____

NOTES: _____

_____

_____

WEBSITE URL: _____

USERNAME: _____

PASSWORD: _____

HINT: _____

NOTES: _____

_____

WEBSITE URL: _____

USERNAME: _____

PASSWORD: _____

HINT: _____

NOTES: _____

_____

WEBSITE URL: _____

USERNAME: _____

PASSWORD: _____

HINT: _____

NOTES: _____

_____

WEBSITE URL: _____

USERNAME: _____

PASSWORD: _____

HINT: _____

NOTES: _____

_____

_____

WEBSITE URL: _____

USERNAME: _____

PASSWORD: _____

HINT: _____

NOTES: _____

_____

WEBSITE URL: _____

USERNAME: _____

PASSWORD: _____

HINT: _____

NOTES: _____

_____

WEBSITE URL: _____

USERNAME: _____

PASSWORD: _____

HINT: _____

NOTES: _____

_____

WEBSITE URL: _____

USERNAME: _____

PASSWORD: _____

HINT: _____

NOTES: _____

_____

_____

WEBSITE URL: _____

USERNAME: _____

PASSWORD: _____

HINT: _____

NOTES: _____

_____

WEBSITE URL: _____

USERNAME: _____

PASSWORD: _____

HINT: _____

NOTES: _____

_____

WEBSITE URL: _____

USERNAME: _____

PASSWORD: _____

HINT: _____

NOTES: _____

_____

WEBSITE URL: _____

USERNAME: _____

PASSWORD: _____

HINT: _____

NOTES: _____

_____

_____

WEBSITE URL: _____

USERNAME: _____

PASSWORD: _____

HINT: _____

NOTES: _____

_____

WEBSITE URL: _____

USERNAME: _____

PASSWORD: _____

HINT: _____

NOTES: _____

_____

WEBSITE URL: _____

USERNAME: _____

PASSWORD: _____

HINT: _____

NOTES: _____

_____

WEBSITE URL: _____

USERNAME: _____

PASSWORD: _____

HINT: _____

NOTES: _____

_____

_____

WEBSITE URL: _____

USERNAME: _____

PASSWORD: _____

HINT: _____

NOTES: _____

_____

WEBSITE URL: _____

USERNAME: _____

PASSWORD: _____

HINT: _____

NOTES: _____

_____

WEBSITE URL: _____

USERNAME: _____

PASSWORD: _____

HINT: _____

NOTES: _____

_____

WEBSITE URL: _____

USERNAME: _____

PASSWORD: _____

HINT: _____

NOTES: _____

_____

_____

WEBSITE URL: _____

USERNAME: _____

PASSWORD: _____

HINT: _____

NOTES: _____

_____

WEBSITE URL: _____

USERNAME: _____

PASSWORD: _____

HINT: _____

NOTES: _____

_____

WEBSITE URL: _____

USERNAME: _____

PASSWORD: _____

HINT: _____

NOTES: _____

_____

WEBSITE URL: _____

USERNAME: _____

PASSWORD: _____

HINT: _____

NOTES: _____

_____

_____

WEBSITE URL: _____

USERNAME: _____

PASSWORD: _____

HINT: _____

NOTES: _____

_____

WEBSITE URL: _____

USERNAME: _____

PASSWORD: _____

HINT: _____

NOTES: _____

_____

WEBSITE URL: _____

USERNAME: _____

PASSWORD: _____

HINT: _____

NOTES: _____

_____

WEBSITE URL: _____

USERNAME: _____

PASSWORD: _____

HINT: _____

NOTES: _____

_____

_____

WEBSITE URL: _____

USERNAME: _____

PASSWORD: _____

HINT: _____

NOTES: _____

_____

WEBSITE URL: _____

USERNAME: _____

PASSWORD: _____

HINT: _____

NOTES: _____

_____

WEBSITE URL: _____

USERNAME: _____

PASSWORD: _____

HINT: _____

NOTES: _____

_____

WEBSITE URL: _____

USERNAME: _____

PASSWORD: _____

HINT: _____

NOTES: _____

_____

_____

WEBSITE URL: _____

USERNAME: _____

PASSWORD: _____

HINT: _____

NOTES: _____

_____

WEBSITE URL: _____

USERNAME: _____

PASSWORD: _____

HINT: _____

NOTES: _____

_____

WEBSITE URL: _____

USERNAME: _____

PASSWORD: _____

HINT: _____

NOTES: _____

_____

WEBSITE URL: _____

USERNAME: _____

PASSWORD: _____

HINT: _____

NOTES: _____

_____

_____

WEBSITE URL: _____

USERNAME: _____

PASSWORD: _____

HINT: _____

NOTES: _____

_____

WEBSITE URL: _____

USERNAME: _____

PASSWORD: _____

HINT: _____

NOTES: _____

_____

WEBSITE URL: _____

USERNAME: _____

PASSWORD: _____

HINT: _____

NOTES: _____

_____

WEBSITE URL: _____

USERNAME: _____

PASSWORD: _____

HINT: _____

NOTES: _____

_____

_____

WEBSITE URL: _____

USERNAME: _____

PASSWORD: _____

HINT: _____

NOTES: _____

_____

WEBSITE URL: _____

USERNAME: _____

PASSWORD: _____

HINT: _____

NOTES: _____

_____

WEBSITE URL: _____

USERNAME: _____

PASSWORD: _____

HINT: _____

NOTES: _____

_____

WEBSITE URL: _____

USERNAME: _____

PASSWORD: _____

HINT: _____

NOTES: _____

_____

_____

WEBSITE URL: _____

USERNAME: _____

PASSWORD: _____

HINT: _____

NOTES: _____

_____

WEBSITE URL: _____

USERNAME: _____

PASSWORD: _____

HINT: _____

NOTES: _____

_____

WEBSITE URL: _____

USERNAME: _____

PASSWORD: _____

HINT: _____

NOTES: _____

_____

WEBSITE URL: _____

USERNAME: _____

PASSWORD: _____

HINT: _____

NOTES: _____

_____

_____

WEBSITE URL: _____

USERNAME: _____

PASSWORD: _____

HINT: _____

NOTES: _____

_____

WEBSITE URL: _____

USERNAME: _____

PASSWORD: _____

HINT: _____

NOTES: _____

_____

WEBSITE URL: _____

USERNAME: _____

PASSWORD: _____

HINT: _____

NOTES: _____

_____

WEBSITE URL: _____

USERNAME: _____

PASSWORD: _____

HINT: _____

NOTES: _____

_____

_____

WEBSITE URL: _____

USERNAME: _____

PASSWORD: _____

HINT: _____

NOTES: _____

_____

WEBSITE URL: _____

USERNAME: _____

PASSWORD: _____

HINT: _____

NOTES: _____

_____

WEBSITE URL: _____

USERNAME: _____

PASSWORD: _____

HINT: _____

NOTES: _____

_____

WEBSITE URL: _____

USERNAME: _____

PASSWORD: _____

HINT: _____

NOTES: _____

_____

_____

WEBSITE URL: _____

USERNAME: _____

PASSWORD: _____

HINT: _____

NOTES: _____

_____

WEBSITE URL: _____

USERNAME: _____

PASSWORD: _____

HINT: _____

NOTES: _____

_____

WEBSITE URL: _____

USERNAME: _____

PASSWORD: _____

HINT: _____

NOTES: _____

_____

WEBSITE URL: _____

USERNAME: _____

PASSWORD: _____

HINT: _____

NOTES: _____

_____

_____

WEBSITE URL: _____

USERNAME: _____

PASSWORD: _____

HINT: _____

NOTES: _____

_____

WEBSITE URL: _____

USERNAME: _____

PASSWORD: _____

HINT: _____

NOTES: _____

_____

WEBSITE URL: _____

USERNAME: _____

PASSWORD: _____

HINT: _____

NOTES: _____

_____

WEBSITE URL: _____

USERNAME: _____

PASSWORD: _____

HINT: _____

NOTES: _____

_____

_____

WEBSITE URL: _____

USERNAME: _____

PASSWORD: _____

HINT: _____

NOTES: _____

_____

WEBSITE URL: _____

USERNAME: _____

PASSWORD: _____

HINT: _____

NOTES: _____

_____

WEBSITE URL: _____

USERNAME: _____

PASSWORD: _____

HINT: _____

NOTES: _____

_____

WEBSITE URL: _____

USERNAME: _____

PASSWORD: _____

HINT: _____

NOTES: _____

_____

_____

WEBSITE URL: _____

USERNAME: _____

PASSWORD: _____

HINT: _____

NOTES: _____

_____

WEBSITE URL: _____

USERNAME: _____

PASSWORD: _____

HINT: _____

NOTES: _____

_____

WEBSITE URL: _____

USERNAME: _____

PASSWORD: _____

HINT: _____

NOTES: _____

_____

WEBSITE URL: _____

USERNAME: _____

PASSWORD: _____

HINT: _____

NOTES: _____

_____

_____

WEBSITE URL: _____

USERNAME: _____

PASSWORD: _____

HINT: _____

NOTES: _____

_____

WEBSITE URL: _____

USERNAME: _____

PASSWORD: _____

HINT: _____

NOTES: _____

_____

WEBSITE URL: _____

USERNAME: _____

PASSWORD: _____

HINT: _____

NOTES: _____

_____

WEBSITE URL: _____

USERNAME: _____

PASSWORD: _____

HINT: _____

NOTES: _____

_____

_____

WEBSITE URL: _____

USERNAME: _____

PASSWORD: _____

HINT: _____

NOTES: _____

_____

WEBSITE URL: _____

USERNAME: _____

PASSWORD: _____

HINT: _____

NOTES: _____

_____

WEBSITE URL: _____

USERNAME: _____

PASSWORD: _____

HINT: _____

NOTES: _____

_____

WEBSITE URL: _____

USERNAME: _____

PASSWORD: _____

HINT: _____

NOTES: _____

_____

_____

WEBSITE URL: _____

USERNAME: _____

PASSWORD: _____

HINT: _____

NOTES: _____

_____

WEBSITE URL: _____

USERNAME: _____

PASSWORD: _____

HINT: _____

NOTES: _____

_____

WEBSITE URL: _____

USERNAME: _____

PASSWORD: _____

HINT: _____

NOTES: _____

_____

WEBSITE URL: _____

USERNAME: _____

PASSWORD: _____

HINT: _____

NOTES: _____

_____

_____

WEBSITE URL: _____

USERNAME: _____

PASSWORD: _____

HINT: _____

NOTES: _____

_____

WEBSITE URL: _____

USERNAME: _____

PASSWORD: _____

HINT: _____

NOTES: _____

_____

WEBSITE URL: _____

USERNAME: _____

PASSWORD: _____

HINT: _____

NOTES: _____

_____

WEBSITE URL: _____

USERNAME: _____

PASSWORD: _____

HINT: _____

NOTES: _____

_____

_____

WEBSITE URL: _____

USERNAME: _____

PASSWORD: _____

HINT: _____

NOTES: _____

_____

WEBSITE URL: _____

USERNAME: _____

PASSWORD: _____

HINT: _____

NOTES: _____

_____

WEBSITE URL: _____

USERNAME: _____

PASSWORD: _____

HINT: _____

NOTES: _____

_____

WEBSITE URL: _____

USERNAME: _____

PASSWORD: _____

HINT: _____

NOTES: _____

_____

_____

WEBSITE URL: _____

USERNAME: _____

PASSWORD: _____

HINT: _____

NOTES: _____

_____

WEBSITE URL: _____

USERNAME: _____

PASSWORD: _____

HINT: _____

NOTES: _____

_____

WEBSITE URL: _____

USERNAME: _____

PASSWORD: _____

HINT: _____

NOTES: _____

_____

WEBSITE URL: _____

USERNAME: _____

PASSWORD: _____

HINT: _____

NOTES: _____

_____

_____

WEBSITE URL: _____

USERNAME: _____

PASSWORD: _____

HINT: _____

NOTES: _____

_____

WEBSITE URL: _____

USERNAME: _____

PASSWORD: _____

HINT: _____

NOTES: _____

_____

WEBSITE URL: _____

USERNAME: _____

PASSWORD: _____

HINT: _____

NOTES: _____

_____

WEBSITE URL: _____

USERNAME: _____

PASSWORD: _____

HINT: _____

NOTES: _____

_____

_____

WEBSITE URL: _____

USERNAME: _____

PASSWORD: _____

HINT: _____

NOTES: _____

_____

WEBSITE URL: _____

USERNAME: _____

PASSWORD: _____

HINT: _____

NOTES: _____

_____

WEBSITE URL: _____

USERNAME: _____

PASSWORD: _____

HINT: _____

NOTES: _____

_____

WEBSITE URL: _____

USERNAME: _____

PASSWORD: _____

HINT: _____

NOTES: _____

_____

_____

WEBSITE URL: _____

USERNAME: _____

PASSWORD: _____

HINT: _____

NOTES: _____

_____

WEBSITE URL: _____

USERNAME: _____

PASSWORD: _____

HINT: _____

NOTES: _____

_____

WEBSITE URL: _____

USERNAME: _____

PASSWORD: _____

HINT: _____

NOTES: _____

_____

WEBSITE URL: _____

USERNAME: _____

PASSWORD: _____

HINT: _____

NOTES: _____

_____

_____

WEBSITE URL: _____

USERNAME: _____

PASSWORD: _____

HINT: _____

NOTES: _____

_____

WEBSITE URL: _____

USERNAME: _____

PASSWORD: _____

HINT: _____

NOTES: _____

_____

WEBSITE URL: _____

USERNAME: _____

PASSWORD: _____

HINT: _____

NOTES: _____

_____

WEBSITE URL: _____

USERNAME: _____

PASSWORD: _____

HINT: _____

NOTES: _____

_____

_____

WEBSITE URL: _____

USERNAME: _____

PASSWORD: _____

HINT: _____

NOTES: _____

_____

WEBSITE URL: _____

USERNAME: _____

PASSWORD: _____

HINT: _____

NOTES: _____

_____

WEBSITE URL: _____

USERNAME: _____

PASSWORD: _____

HINT: _____

NOTES: _____

_____

WEBSITE URL: _____

USERNAME: _____

PASSWORD: _____

HINT: _____

NOTES: _____

_____

_____

WEBSITE URL: _____

USERNAME: _____

PASSWORD: _____

HINT: _____

NOTES: _____

_____

WEBSITE URL: _____

USERNAME: _____

PASSWORD: _____

HINT: _____

NOTES: _____

_____

WEBSITE URL: _____

USERNAME: _____

PASSWORD: _____

HINT: _____

NOTES: _____

_____

WEBSITE URL: _____

USERNAME: _____

PASSWORD: _____

HINT: _____

NOTES: _____

_____

_____

WEBSITE URL: _____

USERNAME: _____

PASSWORD: _____

HINT: _____

NOTES: _____

_____

WEBSITE URL: _____

USERNAME: _____

PASSWORD: _____

HINT: _____

NOTES: _____

_____

WEBSITE URL: _____

USERNAME: _____

PASSWORD: _____

HINT: _____

NOTES: _____

_____

WEBSITE URL: _____

USERNAME: _____

PASSWORD: _____

HINT: _____

NOTES: _____

_____

_____

WEBSITE URL: _____

USERNAME: _____

PASSWORD: _____

HINT: _____

NOTES: _____

_____

WEBSITE URL: _____

USERNAME: _____

PASSWORD: _____

HINT: _____

NOTES: _____

_____

WEBSITE URL: _____

USERNAME: _____

PASSWORD: _____

HINT: _____

NOTES: _____

_____

WEBSITE URL: _____

USERNAME: _____

PASSWORD: _____

HINT: _____

NOTES: _____

_____

_____

WEBSITE URL: _____

USERNAME: _____

PASSWORD: _____

HINT: _____

NOTES: _____

_____

WEBSITE URL: _____

USERNAME: _____

PASSWORD: _____

HINT: _____

NOTES: _____

_____

WEBSITE URL: _____

USERNAME: _____

PASSWORD: _____

HINT: _____

NOTES: _____

_____

WEBSITE URL: _____

USERNAME: _____

PASSWORD: _____

HINT: _____

NOTES: _____

_____

_____

WEBSITE URL: _____

USERNAME: _____

PASSWORD: _____

HINT: _____

NOTES: _____

_____

WEBSITE URL: _____

USERNAME: _____

PASSWORD: _____

HINT: _____

NOTES: _____

_____

WEBSITE URL: _____

USERNAME: _____

PASSWORD: _____

HINT: _____

NOTES: _____

_____

WEBSITE URL: _____

USERNAME: _____

PASSWORD: _____

HINT: _____

NOTES: _____

_____

_____

WEBSITE URL: _____

USERNAME: _____

PASSWORD: _____

HINT: _____

NOTES: _____

_____

WEBSITE URL: _____

USERNAME: _____

PASSWORD: _____

HINT: _____

NOTES: _____

_____

WEBSITE URL: _____

USERNAME: _____

PASSWORD: _____

HINT: _____

NOTES: _____

_____

WEBSITE URL: _____

USERNAME: _____

PASSWORD: _____

HINT: _____

NOTES: _____

_____

_____

WEBSITE URL: _____

USERNAME: _____

PASSWORD: _____

HINT: _____

NOTES: _____

_____

WEBSITE URL: _____

USERNAME: _____

PASSWORD: _____

HINT: _____

NOTES: _____

_____

WEBSITE URL: _____

USERNAME: _____

PASSWORD: _____

HINT: _____

NOTES: _____

_____

WEBSITE URL: _____

USERNAME: _____

PASSWORD: _____

HINT: _____

NOTES: _____

_____

_____

WEBSITE URL: _____

USERNAME: _____

PASSWORD: _____

HINT: _____

NOTES: _____

_____

WEBSITE URL: _____

USERNAME: _____

PASSWORD: _____

HINT: _____

NOTES: _____

_____

WEBSITE URL: _____

USERNAME: _____

PASSWORD: _____

HINT: _____

NOTES: _____

_____

WEBSITE URL: _____

USERNAME: _____

PASSWORD: _____

HINT: _____

NOTES: _____

_____

_____

WEBSITE URL: _____

USERNAME: _____

PASSWORD: _____

HINT: _____

NOTES: _____

_____

WEBSITE URL: _____

USERNAME: _____

PASSWORD: _____

HINT: _____

NOTES: _____

_____

WEBSITE URL: _____

USERNAME: _____

PASSWORD: _____

HINT: _____

NOTES: _____

_____

WEBSITE URL: _____

USERNAME: _____

PASSWORD: _____

HINT: _____

NOTES: _____

_____

_____

WEBSITE URL: _____

USERNAME: _____

PASSWORD: _____

HINT: _____

NOTES: _____

_____

WEBSITE URL: _____

USERNAME: _____

PASSWORD: _____

HINT: _____

NOTES: _____

_____

WEBSITE URL: _____

USERNAME: _____

PASSWORD: _____

HINT: _____

NOTES: _____

_____

WEBSITE URL: _____

USERNAME: _____

PASSWORD: _____

HINT: _____

NOTES: _____

_____

_____

WEBSITE URL: _____

USERNAME: _____

PASSWORD: _____

HINT: _____

NOTES: _____

_____

WEBSITE URL: _____

USERNAME: _____

PASSWORD: _____

HINT: _____

NOTES: _____

_____

WEBSITE URL: _____

USERNAME: _____

PASSWORD: _____

HINT: _____

NOTES: _____

_____

WEBSITE URL: _____

USERNAME: _____

PASSWORD: _____

HINT: _____

NOTES: _____

_____

_____

WEBSITE URL: _____

USERNAME: _____

PASSWORD: _____

HINT: _____

NOTES: _____

_____

WEBSITE URL: _____

USERNAME: _____

PASSWORD: _____

HINT: _____

NOTES: _____

_____

WEBSITE URL: _____

USERNAME: _____

PASSWORD: _____

HINT: _____

NOTES: _____

_____

WEBSITE URL: _____

USERNAME: _____

PASSWORD: _____

HINT: _____

NOTES: _____

_____

_____

WEBSITE URL: _____

USERNAME: _____

PASSWORD: _____

HINT: _____

NOTES: _____

_____

WEBSITE URL: _____

USERNAME: _____

PASSWORD: _____

HINT: _____

NOTES: _____

_____

WEBSITE URL: _____

USERNAME: _____

PASSWORD: _____

HINT: _____

NOTES: _____

_____

WEBSITE URL: _____

USERNAME: _____

PASSWORD: _____

HINT: _____

NOTES: _____

_____

_____

WEBSITE URL: _____

USERNAME: _____

PASSWORD: _____

HINT: _____

NOTES: _____

_____

WEBSITE URL: _____

USERNAME: _____

PASSWORD: _____

HINT: _____

NOTES: _____

_____

WEBSITE URL: _____

USERNAME: _____

PASSWORD: _____

HINT: _____

NOTES: _____

_____

WEBSITE URL: _____

USERNAME: _____

PASSWORD: _____

HINT: _____

NOTES: _____

_____

_____

WEBSITE URL: _____

USERNAME: _____

PASSWORD: _____

HINT: _____

NOTES: _____

_____

WEBSITE URL: _____

USERNAME: _____

PASSWORD: _____

HINT: _____

NOTES: _____

_____

WEBSITE URL: _____

USERNAME: _____

PASSWORD: _____

HINT: _____

NOTES: _____

_____

WEBSITE URL: _____

USERNAME: _____

PASSWORD: _____

HINT: _____

NOTES: _____

_____

_____

WEBSITE URL: _____

USERNAME: _____

PASSWORD: _____

HINT: _____

NOTES: _____

_____

WEBSITE URL: _____

USERNAME: _____

PASSWORD: _____

HINT: _____

NOTES: _____

_____

WEBSITE URL: _____

USERNAME: _____

PASSWORD: _____

HINT: _____

NOTES: _____

_____

WEBSITE URL: _____

USERNAME: _____

PASSWORD: _____

HINT: _____

NOTES: _____

_____

_____

WEBSITE URL: _____

USERNAME: _____

PASSWORD: _____

HINT: _____

NOTES: _____

_____

WEBSITE URL: _____

USERNAME: _____

PASSWORD: _____

HINT: _____

NOTES: _____

_____

WEBSITE URL: _____

USERNAME: _____

PASSWORD: _____

HINT: _____

NOTES: _____

_____

WEBSITE URL: _____

USERNAME: _____

PASSWORD: _____

HINT: _____

NOTES: _____

_____

_____

WEBSITE URL: _____

USERNAME: _____

PASSWORD: _____

HINT: _____

NOTES: _____

_____

WEBSITE URL: _____

USERNAME: _____

PASSWORD: _____

HINT: _____

NOTES: _____

_____

WEBSITE URL: _____

USERNAME: _____

PASSWORD: _____

HINT: _____

NOTES: _____

_____

WEBSITE URL: _____

USERNAME: _____

PASSWORD: _____

HINT: _____

NOTES: _____

_____

_____

WEBSITE URL: _____

USERNAME: _____

PASSWORD: _____

HINT: _____

NOTES: _____

_____

WEBSITE URL: _____

USERNAME: _____

PASSWORD: _____

HINT: _____

NOTES: _____

_____

WEBSITE URL: _____

USERNAME: _____

PASSWORD: _____

HINT: _____

NOTES: _____

_____

WEBSITE URL: _____

USERNAME: _____

PASSWORD: _____

HINT: _____

NOTES: _____

_____

WEBSITE URL: _____

USERNAME: _____

PASSWORD: _____

HINT: _____

NOTES: _____

_____

WEBSITE URL: _____

USERNAME: _____

PASSWORD: _____

HINT: _____

NOTES: _____

_____

WEBSITE URL: _____

USERNAME: _____

PASSWORD: _____

HINT: _____

NOTES: _____

_____

WEBSITE URL: _____

USERNAME: _____

PASSWORD: _____

HINT: _____

NOTES: _____

_____

_____

WEBSITE URL: _____

USERNAME: _____

PASSWORD: _____

HINT: _____

NOTES: _____

_____

WEBSITE URL: _____

USERNAME: _____

PASSWORD: _____

HINT: _____

NOTES: _____

_____

WEBSITE URL: _____

USERNAME: _____

PASSWORD: _____

HINT: _____

NOTES: _____

_____

WEBSITE URL: _____

USERNAME: _____

PASSWORD: _____

HINT: _____

NOTES: _____

_____

_____

WEBSITE URL: _____

USERNAME: _____

PASSWORD: _____

HINT: _____

NOTES: _____

_____

WEBSITE URL: _____

USERNAME: _____

PASSWORD: _____

HINT: _____

NOTES: _____

_____

WEBSITE URL: _____

USERNAME: _____

PASSWORD: _____

HINT: _____

NOTES: _____

_____

WEBSITE URL: _____

USERNAME: _____

PASSWORD: _____

HINT: _____

NOTES: _____

_____

_____

WEBSITE URL: _____

USERNAME: _____

PASSWORD: _____

HINT: _____

NOTES: _____

_____

WEBSITE URL: _____

USERNAME: _____

PASSWORD: _____

HINT: _____

NOTES: _____

_____

WEBSITE URL: _____

USERNAME: _____

PASSWORD: _____

HINT: _____

NOTES: _____

_____

WEBSITE URL: _____

USERNAME: _____

PASSWORD: _____

HINT: _____

NOTES: _____

_____

_____

WEBSITE URL: _____

USERNAME: _____

PASSWORD: _____

HINT: _____

NOTES: _____

_____

WEBSITE URL: _____

USERNAME: _____

PASSWORD: _____

HINT: _____

NOTES: _____

_____

WEBSITE URL: _____

USERNAME: _____

PASSWORD: _____

HINT: _____

NOTES: _____

_____

WEBSITE URL: _____

USERNAME: _____

PASSWORD: _____

HINT: _____

NOTES: _____

_____

_____

WEBSITE URL: _____

USERNAME: _____

PASSWORD: _____

HINT: _____

NOTES: _____

_____

WEBSITE URL: _____

USERNAME: _____

PASSWORD: _____

HINT: _____

NOTES: _____

_____

WEBSITE URL: _____

USERNAME: _____

PASSWORD: _____

HINT: _____

NOTES: _____

_____

WEBSITE URL: _____

USERNAME: _____

PASSWORD: _____

HINT: _____

NOTES: _____

_____

WEBSITE URL: _____

USERNAME: _____

PASSWORD: _____

HINT: _____

NOTES: _____

_____

WEBSITE URL: _____

USERNAME: _____

PASSWORD: _____

HINT: _____

NOTES: _____

_____

WEBSITE URL: _____

USERNAME: _____

PASSWORD: _____

HINT: _____

NOTES: _____

_____

WEBSITE URL: _____

USERNAME: _____

PASSWORD: _____

HINT: _____

NOTES: _____

_____

_____

WEBSITE URL: _____

USERNAME: _____

PASSWORD: _____

HINT: _____

NOTES: _____

_____

WEBSITE URL: _____

USERNAME: _____

PASSWORD: _____

HINT: _____

NOTES: _____

_____

WEBSITE URL: _____

USERNAME: _____

PASSWORD: _____

HINT: _____

NOTES: _____

_____

WEBSITE URL: _____

USERNAME: _____

PASSWORD: _____

HINT: _____

NOTES: _____

_____

_____

WEBSITE URL: _____

USERNAME: _____

PASSWORD: _____

HINT: _____

NOTES: _____

_____

WEBSITE URL: _____

USERNAME: _____

PASSWORD: _____

HINT: _____

NOTES: _____

_____

WEBSITE URL: _____

USERNAME: _____

PASSWORD: _____

HINT: _____

NOTES: _____

_____

WEBSITE URL: _____

USERNAME: _____

PASSWORD: _____

HINT: _____

NOTES: _____

_____

_____

WEBSITE URL: _____

USERNAME: _____

PASSWORD: _____

HINT: _____

NOTES: _____

_____

WEBSITE URL: _____

USERNAME: _____

PASSWORD: _____

HINT: _____

NOTES: _____

_____

WEBSITE URL: _____

USERNAME: _____

PASSWORD: _____

HINT: _____

NOTES: _____

_____

WEBSITE URL: _____

USERNAME: _____

PASSWORD: _____

HINT: _____

NOTES: _____

_____

_____

WEBSITE URL: _____

USERNAME: _____

PASSWORD: _____

HINT: _____

NOTES: _____

_____

WEBSITE URL: _____

USERNAME: _____

PASSWORD: _____

HINT: _____

NOTES: _____

_____

WEBSITE URL: _____

USERNAME: _____

PASSWORD: _____

HINT: _____

NOTES: _____

_____

WEBSITE URL: _____

USERNAME: _____

PASSWORD: _____

HINT: _____

NOTES: _____

_____

_____

WEBSITE URL: _____

USERNAME: _____

PASSWORD: _____

HINT: _____

NOTES: _____

_____

WEBSITE URL: _____

USERNAME: _____

PASSWORD: _____

HINT: _____

NOTES: _____

_____

WEBSITE URL: _____

USERNAME: _____

PASSWORD: _____

HINT: _____

NOTES: _____

_____

WEBSITE URL: _____

USERNAME: _____

PASSWORD: _____

HINT: _____

NOTES: _____

_____

WEBSITE URL: _____

USERNAME: _____

PASSWORD: _____

HINT: _____

NOTES: _____

_____

WEBSITE URL: _____

USERNAME: _____

PASSWORD: _____

HINT: _____

NOTES: _____

_____

WEBSITE URL: _____

USERNAME: _____

PASSWORD: _____

HINT: _____

NOTES: _____

_____

WEBSITE URL: _____

USERNAME: _____

PASSWORD: _____

HINT: _____

NOTES: _____

_____

_____

WEBSITE URL: _____

USERNAME: _____

PASSWORD: _____

HINT: _____

NOTES: _____

_____

WEBSITE URL: _____

USERNAME: _____

PASSWORD: _____

HINT: _____

NOTES: _____

_____

WEBSITE URL: _____

USERNAME: _____

PASSWORD: _____

HINT: _____

NOTES: _____

_____

WEBSITE URL: _____

USERNAME: _____

PASSWORD: _____

HINT: _____

NOTES: _____

_____

_____

WEBSITE URL: _____

USERNAME: _____

PASSWORD: _____

HINT: _____

NOTES: _____

_____

WEBSITE URL: _____

USERNAME: _____

PASSWORD: _____

HINT: _____

NOTES: _____

_____

WEBSITE URL: _____

USERNAME: _____

PASSWORD: _____

HINT: _____

NOTES: _____

_____

WEBSITE URL: _____

USERNAME: _____

PASSWORD: _____

HINT: _____

NOTES: _____

_____

_____

WEBSITE URL: _____

USERNAME: _____

PASSWORD: _____

HINT: _____

NOTES: _____

_____

WEBSITE URL: _____

USERNAME: _____

PASSWORD: _____

HINT: _____

NOTES: _____

_____

WEBSITE URL: _____

USERNAME: _____

PASSWORD: _____

HINT: _____

NOTES: _____

_____

WEBSITE URL: _____

USERNAME: _____

PASSWORD: _____

HINT: _____

NOTES: _____

_____

_____

WEBSITE URL: _____

USERNAME: _____

PASSWORD: _____

HINT: _____

NOTES: _____

_____

WEBSITE URL: _____

USERNAME: _____

PASSWORD: _____

HINT: _____

NOTES: _____

_____

WEBSITE URL: _____

USERNAME: _____

PASSWORD: _____

HINT: _____

NOTES: _____

_____

WEBSITE URL: _____

USERNAME: _____

PASSWORD: _____

HINT: _____

NOTES: _____

_____

_____

WEBSITE URL: _____

USERNAME: _____

PASSWORD: _____

HINT: _____

NOTES: _____

_____

WEBSITE URL: _____

USERNAME: _____

PASSWORD: _____

HINT: _____

NOTES: _____

_____

WEBSITE URL: _____

USERNAME: _____

PASSWORD: _____

HINT: _____

NOTES: _____

_____

WEBSITE URL: _____

USERNAME: _____

PASSWORD: _____

HINT: _____

NOTES: _____

_____

_____

WEBSITE URL: _____

USERNAME: _____

PASSWORD: _____

HINT: _____

NOTES: _____

_____

WEBSITE URL: _____

USERNAME: _____

PASSWORD: _____

HINT: _____

NOTES: _____

_____

WEBSITE URL: _____

USERNAME: _____

PASSWORD: _____

HINT: _____

NOTES: _____

_____

WEBSITE URL: _____

USERNAME: _____

PASSWORD: _____

HINT: _____

NOTES: _____

_____

_____

WEBSITE URL: _____

USERNAME: _____

PASSWORD: _____

HINT: _____

NOTES: _____

_____

WEBSITE URL: _____

USERNAME: _____

PASSWORD: _____

HINT: _____

NOTES: _____

_____

WEBSITE URL: _____

USERNAME: _____

PASSWORD: _____

HINT: _____

NOTES: _____

_____

WEBSITE URL: _____

USERNAME: _____

PASSWORD: _____

HINT: _____

NOTES: _____

_____

_____

CPSIA information can be obtained
at www.ICGtesting.com
Printed in the USA
LVHW010228200423
744877LV00012B/108